SCOTT MYLES
THIS PRODUCTION

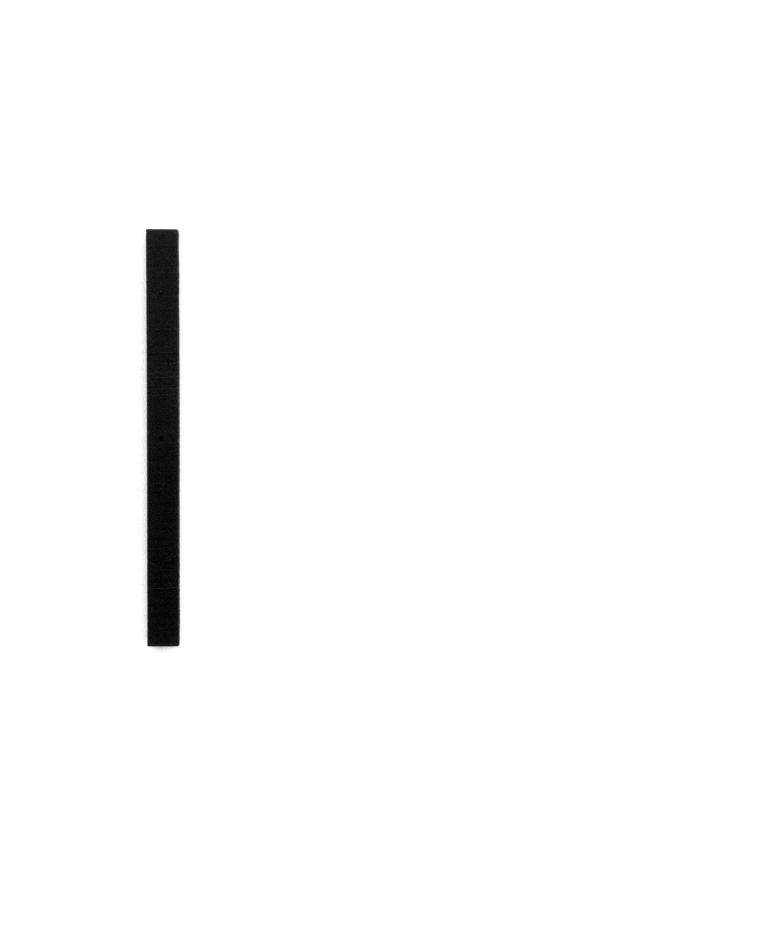

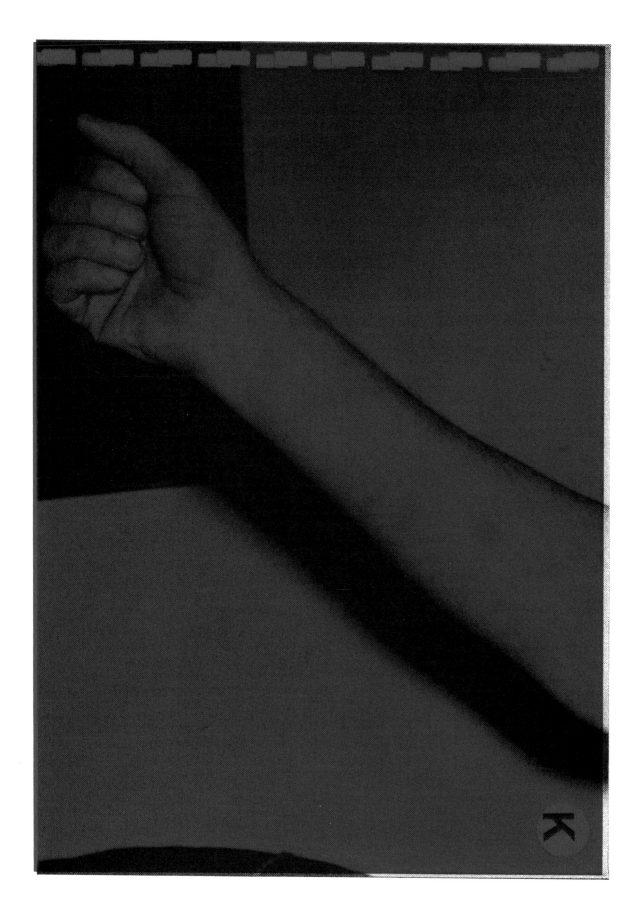

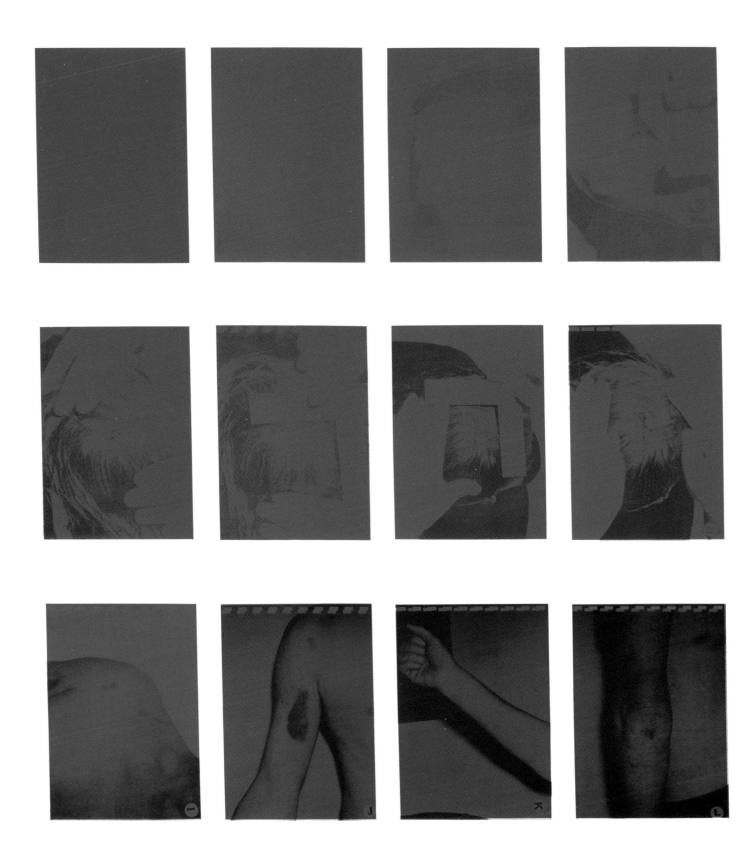

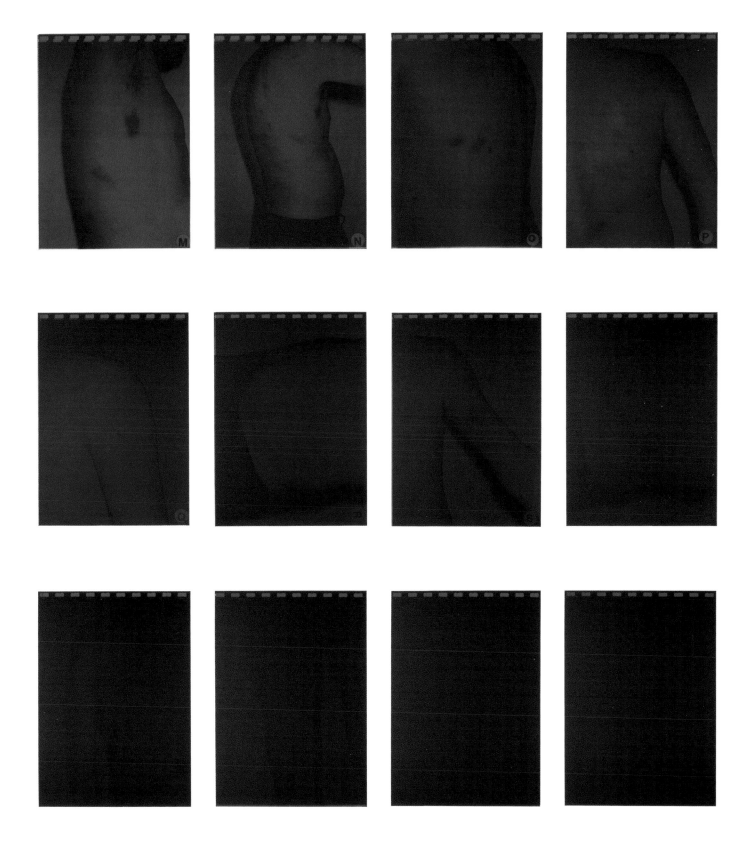

ELBA

ELBA

Manilla Wallet

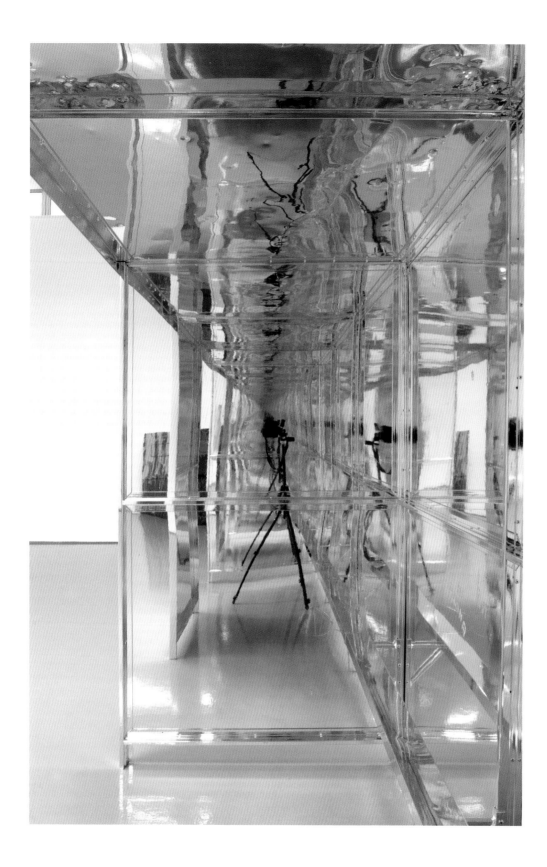

'Houses in Motion…'

Dominic Paterson

According to a well-known metaphor, the novelist demolishes the house of his life and uses its bricks to construct another house: that of his novel. From which it follows that a novelist's biographers unmake what the novelist made, and remake what he unmade. Their labour, from the standpoint of art utterly negative, can illuminate neither the value nor the meaning of a novel.
Milan Kundera, *The Art of the Novel* [1]

To great writers finished works weigh lighter than those fragments on which they work throughout their lives. For only the more feeble and distracted take an inimitable pleasure in closure, feeling that their lives have thereby been given back to them.
Walter Benjamin, *One-Way Street* [2]

As an interpretive angle from which to explore Scott Myles's *This Production*, the theme of the construction and deconstruction of houses is provisional, but not arbitrary. The above epigraph from Kundera, with its pointed take on artistic and critical making and unmaking of the 'houses' of life and art, was explicitly invoked by the artist in relation to the exhibition, and resonances with the activity of building and with its materials could certainly be felt throughout the works shown at DCA. Take, for example, *STABILA (Black and Blue)*, (2012), a series of prints which reproduce court photographs ('productions') showing the injuries sustained by a man beaten with a STABILA-branded spirit level after an argument with a co-worker on a building site. Shifting across the numbered series from blue to black, these images are both evidentiary and bodily, as if the indexical photograph were itself a bruised skin surface. They also play on the disparity between the intended function of a spirit level as a device for correctly aligning objects (in the gallery as much as on the building site) and the violent use to which it was put in this case. Domestic architecture and furnishings were also recollected in *Houdini* (2012), a cast of a bay window which renders opaque a structure designed precisely to be seen through, and in *Flag* (2006), a three-part screen with red, white and blue semi-transparent georgette panels, equally redolent of screenprinting and of museum display, but also suggestive, in scale and function, of bourgeois décor. In all these cases, however, the source material has undergone a process comparable with the 'effacement' to which Jasper Johns subjected everyday objects or iconic images in his paintings and casts, so that the most familiar material of our culture seems to 'exist almost as ruins do,' that is, outwith its original context, and available for the overlaying of new meanings. [3]

In his artistic practice, whether it takes the form of sculptural objects, prints, photographs, installations, or performed actions, Myles seems less interested in fabricating the permanence or stasis we might associate with the house as a figure of the artwork (as in Kundera's 'well-known metaphor'), than in continually reworking the work, keeping it in motion. For Michel Foucault, both author and work, when conceived as whole, continuous, univocal sources of meaning impede 'the free circulation, the free manipulation, the free composition, decomposition, and recomposition of fiction.'[4] Myles's practice, I want to suggest, works through exactly these kinds of processes. It seems necessary to stress this as we turn to the works themselves because they do not trade on any obvious visual registers of incompleteness, decomposition or provisionality; quite the opposite. Prominent amongst the qualities which makes Myles's artistic practice so compelling is the deftness with which he yields conceptual density and semantic openness from markedly concise, elegant forms. If, despite its visual clarity, *This Production* can't be captured by any figure of totality, wholeness or closure, this is not least because Myles's works themselves embody seemingly contradictory qualities, being both simple and complex, mute and eloquent, self-contained and expansive, autonomous and highly contingent.

Couples (2007), one of the first works encountered in *This Production*, neatly demonstrates this. It consists of two identical triangular wooden forms, one serving as a shelf upon which the other is displayed. This simple doubling negates the basic utility we might reasonably expect of a shelf, as the sloping upper surface can no longer function as a support for another object. In place of this utility, one element mirrors the other; the resulting form shows itself showing itself. *Couples*, therefore, seems a model of self-reflexivity, that quality so central to modernist accounts of the autonomy of artworks. But by the same token, in its very doubleness it becomes an 'Un-Shelf,' as Myles puts it, a shelf that is no longer itself. This complexity is extended by the fact that Myles has marbled each form, a chance procedure which makes each unique in appearance: difference displaces self-sameness.

The presentational strategy of using one form as a support for its own mirror image is itself reproduced in other of Myles's works, including two of the last pieces the viewer would encounter in *This Production*, namely *Analysis (Mirror)* (2012), a large new sculpture constructed from two pristinely silvered reclaimed bus shelters, and *Arcade in Vienna* (2005), two marbled shelves which create a non-functional version of a penny arcade. *Couples'* double form, then, is itself doubled by other works otherwise utterly unlike it. Furthermore, as a shelf the form suggests on the one hand the structures of domesticity, and on the other, commercial display: the latter connotation subtly acknowledges the American artist Haim Steinbach's exploration of commodity aesthetics in his well-known shelf works. Finally the title, though at one level simply reflecting the doubleness which constitutes the piece, also alludes to the realm of human relations, to couples and coupling.

Couples, then, has a self-sufficiency which makes one suspect that it is no easier to fix meanings to it than it would be to use it as a shelf. Nevertheless, seen in relation to Myles's wider practice, it might indeed support – or couple with – any or all of the associations just outlined. Like the writing of those, such as Beckett, whom Foucault saw as renouncing the role of the expressive author, *Couples* works by '[r]eferring only to itself, but without being restricted to the confines of its interiority ...': hence its simple complexity.[5]

Another exemplary work in this regard would be *Habitat* (2012), a jesmonite cast of one the eponymous retailer's point-of-sale units which the artist found abandoned. The dismantling of the unit, the addition of some bricks and coins to certain of its elements, the painstaking precision of the casting process, the use of black colouration, and the display of these pieces on the gallery wall, all work to efface the pathos of the found object, its patina of the street, remaking it into something formally abstract, even reminiscent of a constructivist wall relief. It might also suggest the latent potential of flat-packed furniture, awaiting its assembly within the home. Yet with the company's 'home is where the heart is' logo still visible in the cast, *Habitat* could not help but remind the viewer of the fate of that company, most of whose stores were put into administration in 2011. The logo that sought to provoke and capitalise on a desire for home and homeliness thus comes to connote a more downbeat home economy – that of recession, business closures, and the impingement of this financial climate on domestic life. All this underlines the ambiguity of the object's intended function, as a space across which economic transactions and aspirations for the home would once have been discussed: 'a conversation of commerce replaced with a conversation about loss,' Myles suggests.[6]

This kind of mixing or layering of allusions to the art historical, the economic, and the social is a frequent feature of Myles's work. *Interview* (2009–2012), for instance, coaxes a formal echo of Joseph Beuys's famous *Fat Chair* (1963) out of a humble piece of office furniture to which a fabricated Perspex wedge has been fixed. The Perspex in turn supports or holds in space gestural brushstrokes that loosely describe its form. The work also effects an echo of the 'Un-Shelves,' with any unfortunate interviewee sure to slide off, slapstick-style, at the moment they attempt to present themselves for judgement. *Untitled (ELBA grey, black, pink and purple)* and *Untitled (ELBA white and yellow)*, (both 2012), scale up ELBA-branded folders Myles uses to organise his working notes, so that they match his height (194cm) in their width, as if he might be contained by these containers of ideas. Made of paper, the *ELBA* works use screenprinting to approximate both a readymade form redolent of desk work (and perhaps therefore of conceptual art), and to mechanically apply a screenprinted gestural brushstroke, the supposed mark of spontaneous manual creativity.

If subtle references to other artists or artistic paradigms certainly play an important role in Myles's practice, he has also made canny use of more direct appropriations of existing works. Such appropriation is not particularly remarkable in itself, being a widespread feature of contemporary art; what is significant here is the way Myles folds other artists' works into his own artistic language, lending them the ambivalence and complexity which characterises his own work. The ongoing series in which he presents posters by Felix Gonzalez-Torres mounted in custom-made frame structures, sometimes with his own textual or graphic additions on their reverse, work both through a gift economy of exchange, acceptance and reciprocation, and by acknowledging and instantiating the removal from that interpersonal economy of gifting which is effected as soon as they become unique works and enter the logic of museum display.[7]

Displaced Façade (for DCA) (2012) provides a further case in point. The piece is directly modelled on one of nine showrooms designed for the Best hardware chain between 1972 and 1984 by architect James Wines of SITE (Sculpture in the Environment). These astonishingly daring, playful reworkings of the banal spaces of commercial retail, Wines has stated, 'were conceived with the idea of transforming the most familiar design/function/material/construction elements of architecture into an ambiguous commentary on the proper rules of these rhetorically accepted ingredients.'[8] Imitating the Best showroom at Cutler Ridge, Miami, Myles's façade is constructed as if a solid brick wall had been fragmented into three sections. Moving from the first gallery at DCA into the second, the viewer passed through two arch-like gaps afforded in that wall, coming face to face with the smallest section, upon which the screenprint *BOY* (2011) was displayed, almost as if it was a piece of enigmatic commercial signage. Viewed from the back of Gallery 2, the three sections seemed almost to reform into the solid unbroken wall from which they are implicitly taken.

Myles's façade, then, is 'displaced' in several senses. Firstly, and most obviously, as a façade presented inside a gallery, it is displaced from its expected position as the exterior surface of a building.

Insofar as it re-instantiates the Cutler Ridge showroom, it is displaced from another geographical location, while as a recapitulation of an iconic instance of the postmodern architecture of the 1970s and 1980s, it is also somewhat out of time. Here, precisely in *multiple* displacements this work effects, we can begin to discern a distinctive dimension of Myles's approach to appropriation, and its difference from the canonical uses of this strategy made by postmodernists of the 1970s and 1980s, which tended to be either dryly critical of artistic originality, or resignedly celebratory of commodity culture.

As Wines acknowledges, the ideas of Robert Venturi were a crucial influence on the early manifestations of architectural postmodernism, offering a way out of modernist severity via a revalued commercial vernacular. Venturi's 1966 book *Complexity and Contradiction in Architecture* in fact provides a significant point of contact between the Cutler façade and Myles's use of its form, because this text introduces a distinction important to the artist's thinking. 'The tradition 'either-or' has characterized orthodox modern architecture,' Venturi argues: 'a sun screen is probably nothing else; a support is seldom an enclosure.'[9] Against this he sets an 'architecture of complexity and contradiction, which tends to include 'both-and' rather than exclude 'either-or'. It can include elements that are both good and awkward, big and little, closed and open, continuous and articulated, round and square, structural and spatial.'[10] Myles made explicit reference to this inclusive principle in *BOTH AND* (2010), a fluorescent text work included in his 2010 exhibition *ELBA* at Glasgow Print Studio, but it is discernible too in the way many other works layer meanings that might be ordinarily thought to be contradictory, as we have seen.

Another dimension of the logic of 'both-and' relevant to Myles's practice is that which Freud attributes to dreams. 'The alternative '*either-or*' is never expressed in dreams,' Freud writes, 'both of the alternatives being inserted in the text of the dream as though they were equally valid [...] an "either-or" used in recording a dream is to be translated by "and".'[11] And 'displacement' too is, of course, a Freudian term: 'It is the process of displacement which is chiefly responsible for our being unable to discover or recognise the dream-thoughts in the dream-content, unless we understand the reason for their distortion.'[12] The point to be made here is that the 'both-and' logic of postmodern architecture is itself doubled or added to in Myles's work by the intimation of displacing, condensing unconscious processes. In *Analysis (Mirror)*, Myles's second iteration of the double bus shelter form, the lighter burns, scratched names and political slogans, and other marks of their previous use still evident on its immaculate, mirror-like silver surfaces remind us that these were once spaces for waiting, and no doubt for day-dreaming. But they also function as models of an interminable analysis – it is certainly *psychoanalysis* to which the title alludes – because a *mise-en-abyme* effect is produced as they reflect themselves, and the viewer, back and forth across their surfaces. It is as if these fragments of quotidian existence were pieces of a dream that cannot be decoded or deciphered, only endlessly reflected upon.

In 1980, writing on the then nascent emphasis on appropriation and site specificity in the first wave of postmodern art, the critic Craig Owens turned to Walter Benjamin's revaluation of allegory in *The Origin of German Tragic Drama* for a suitable critical model. 'Allegory is consistently attracted to the fragmentary, the imperfect, the incomplete,' Owens wrote, 'an affinity which finds its most comprehensive expression in the ruin, which Benjamin identified as the allegorical emblem par excellence.'[13] Like several of the Best showrooms, the Cutler Ridge façade was constructed as a kind of modern ruin, and Myles's version too had something of this aspect. This again is a temporal displacement, for as Brian Dillon notes, 'the modern ruin is always, to some degree, a palpable, all-too-real remnant of the future.'[14] Interestingly, Dillon gives as an example an oddity that informed *Displaced Façade (for DCA)*, the fact that 'in 1830, having completed his architectural masterpiece, the Bank of England, Sir John Soane commissioned the artist Joseph Gandy to paint a series of views of the structure in ruins.'[15] This past dream of the future takes on a new urgency as it seems to anticipate our own precarious financial era, and Myles's displacement and condensation of the Best façade again accommodates this in its very structure.

Benjamin appropriated allegory and applied its taste for ruins to his own era in order to make 'visibly palpable the experience of a world in fragments.'[16] Thus, in *One-Way Street*, published in 1928, he abandoned the 'pretentious, universal gesture of the book' to present a series of short allegorical fragments that refract the experience of life in inflationary Germany.[17] The fragments often take their titles from urban signage ('This Space for Rent,' 'Post No Bills,' 'Closed for Alterations') – a 'prompt language […] actively equal to the moment.'[18] They also refer to domestic interiors ('Vestibule,' 'Interior Decoration') and the spaces where social and economic transactions take place ('Lost and Found Office,' 'Filling Station,' 'Betting Office'). These fragments aim to use the debris of Benjamin's own historical moment to shatter the 'enervating amazement' which he felt prevented his contemporaries from recognizing the conditions of steady decline which afflicted their society.[19] *One-Way Street* is to this extent like allegory in Baudelaire, which, for Benjamin, 'bears traces of the violence that was necessary to demolish the harmonious façade of the world that surrounded him.'[20]

In the third section of *One-Way Street*, we find an allegorical image for this productive, illuminating demolition work that uncannily recalls the Kundera quote from which the present essay departed. Benjamin writes: 'We have long forgotten the ritual by which the house of our life was erected. But when it is under assault and enemy bombs are already taking their toll, what enervated, perverse antiquities do they not lay bare in the foundations!'[21] Though Benjamin goes on to excavate his own dreams and childhood memories in this allegory, the 'antiquities' to which he refers are not only pieces of his personal history, but preserved traces of the historical origins of the contemporary social order. His hope is to use this material against that order.

In one of the most optimistic sections of *One-Way Street*, Benjamin notes that:

> children are particularly fond of haunting any site where things are being visibly worked on. They are irresistibly drawn by the detritus generated by building, gardening, housework, tailoring, or carpentry … In using these things, they do not so much imitate the works of adults as bring together, in the artifact produced in play, materials of widely differing kinds in a new, intuitive relationship.[22]

As Michael Jennings explains, this is 'a complex political allegory' which combines an image for the 'construction of the Weimar Republic out of the waste products of Empire, out of materials that could not have served the powerful […] with a self-reflexive meditation on the uses of montage.'[23] Self-reflexive because Benjamin's own working procedure was to effect the 'condensation of images made intimate to one another precisely through the impossibility of their affinity.'[24] Political too, because what is at stake in this allegory is the opportunity to not rebuild the collapsed social structures of a failed order, but instead to use their ruins to create something new.

Benjamin's 'construction site' might, then, be taken in turn to allegorise Myles's use of heterogenous materials of all kinds. In his work it is as if the ruins of domestic spaces, urban infrastructure, the studio, the art museum, retail outlets, and so on, were intermingled, and their fragments available to be given new energy and purpose. No work better demonstrates this than the piece Myles made for the Tate Triennial in 2006. Myles arranged that *Untitled (No fire no ashes)*, a 2001 work by Rirkrit Tiravanija consisting of a doorway blocked by cobblestones, be installed at Tate Britain. Tiravanija's work is already dense in historical allusions, to Jannis Kounellis's stone works, and to the famous Situationist slogans of 1968, 'never work' (*ne travaillez jamais*, as inscribed by Tiravanija onto one of the stones) and 'under the cobblestones, the beach'. It was bracketed by Myles's own piece *The End of Summer* (2001) which details in image and text the artist's experience of seeing Tiravanija's work exhibited in Berlin. A photograph shows Myles standing between the work and a slogan which had been graffiti-ed next to it: 'Time is my Capital.' The text concludes by describing seeing the work's de-installation: 'Three men were inside, dismantling the stones and numbering each one, before laying them onto a trailer outside. It felt like the end of summer and time to get back to work.' Myles's work here picks up the elements of his own previous work as well as Tiravanija's to make something else from them, a process akin to what has been termed Benjamin's practice of 'rewriting as superscription; the production of a new text atop the foundations of a previous one.' [25]

At the time of the Triennial, Myles produced a work which was printed in *The Guardian*. These two images, circulating in the daily press, wrote further layers of meaning over the stones Myles had placed in the Tate. It consisted of two photographs: one showing three men amidst the bomb-damaged Duveen galleries during WWII; the other a museum tour guide and visitors standing around Carl Andre's *Equivalent VIII* (1966), the notorious 'Tate bricks'. Two paradigms are thus juxtaposed, a state of ruination awaiting reconstruction and an immaculately self-contained artwork. Though they seem poles apart, Myles knows his work can be 'both-and'. That is why any interpretation, allegorical or otherwise, can only get a hold on this production for so long, before the houses of life and work are in motion once more.

1   Milan Kundera, *The Art of the Novel*, trans. Linda Asher, (London: Faber and Faber, 1999), p.147.

2   Walter Benjamin, *Selected Writings Volume 1, 1913–1926*, ed. Marcus Bullock and Michael W. Jennings, (Cambridge, Massachusetts: Belknap, 1996), p.446.

3   Philip Fisher, *Making and Effacing Art: Modern American Art in a Culture of Museums*, (Cambridge, Massachusetts: Harvard University Press, 1997), p.58.

4   Michel Foucault, 'What is an Author?' in *Essential Works of Foucault, 1954–1984, Volume II: Aesthetics, Method and Epistemology*, ed. James D. Faubion, (London: Allen Lane, 1998), p.221.

5   Ibid, p.206.

6   Correspondence with the author, August 2012.

7   The complexities of gift exchange in these works requires far more extensive treatment than the space of this essay allows. The issue will be taken up in another forthcoming text by the present author.

8   James Wines, 'Arch-Art: Architecture as Subject Matter,' in Glenn Adamson and Jane Pavitt, *Postmodernism: Style and Subversion, 1970–1990*, (London: V&A, 2011), p.103.

9   Robert Venturi, *Complexity and Contradiction in Architecture*, (New York: Museum of Modern Art, 1966), p.23.

10 Ibid.

11 Sigmund Freud, 'On Dreams', *The Standard Edition of the Complete Psychological Works of Sigmund Freud, Vol. V*, trans. James Strachey, (London: Hogarth Press, 1953), p.661.

12 Ibid, p.659.

13 Craig Owens, 'The Allegorical Impulse: Toward a Theory of Postmodernism', in *Beyond Recognition: Representation, Power, and Culture*, (Berkeley and Los Angeles: University of California Press, 1992), p.55.

14 Brian Dillon, 'Fragments from a History of Ruin', *Cabinet*, No. 20, Winter 2005/2006, p.59.

15 Ibid.

16 Susan Buck-Morss, *The Dialectics of Seeing: Walter Benjamin and the Arcades Project*, (Cambridge, Massachusetts: MIT, 1991), p.18.

17 Benjamin, *Selected Writings Volume 1*, p.444.

18 Ibid.

19 Ibid, p.451.

20 Walter Benjamin, *The Arcades Project*, trans. Howard Eiland and Kevin McLaughlin, (Cambridge, Massachusetts: Harvard University Press), [J55a, 3], p.329.

21 Benjamin, *Selected Writings*, p.445.

22 Ibid, pp.449–450.

23 Michael W. Jennings, 'Double Take: Palimpsestic Writing and Image-Character in Benjamin's Late Prose', http://scholar.princeton.edu/jennings/files/jennings_double_take.pdf, (last accessed 20/7/12), p.8.

24 Henry Sussman, 'Between the Registers: The Allegory of Space in Walter Benjamin's Arcades Project', *boundary 2*, Vol. 30, No. 1, Spring 2003, p.174.

25 Jennings, 'Double Take', p.3.

Produced on the occasion of *Scott Myles: This Production* held at Dundee Contemporary Arts

7th April–10th June 2012

Exhibition organised by Graham Domke, assisted by Ewan Wilson and Valerie Norris

Design Robert Dallas Gray

Text Dominic Paterson

Photography Ruth Clark, Alan Dimmick and Scott Myles

Scott Myles and Dundee Contemporary Arts would like to thank:

Scott Campbell, Ruth Clark, Coriander Studio, Robert Dallas Gray, DCA Print Studio, Alan Dimmick, Jan Eugster, Annis Fitzhugh, Claire Forsyth, Nadia Gerazouni, Glasgow Print Studio, Andrew Hamilton, Mike Homer, Simon Hopkins (and Scott Associates), Robert Jackson, David Kordansky, Stuart Krimko, Judith Wylie MacLeod, Jochen Meyer, Thomas Myles, Stephen Norwood, Dominic Paterson, Stathis Panagoulis, Christopher Raymond, Thomas Riegger, Sonia Rosso, Susie Simmons, Sandra Stemmer, Ian Thomson (QD Plastics), George Vamvakidis, Ric Warren, and Toby Webster

Special thanks to everyone at The Breeder, Athens, David Kordansky Gallery, Los Angeles, Meyer Riegger, Berlin and Karlsruhe, The Modern Institute/Toby Webster Ltd, Glasgow, Sonia Rosso (Lira Hotel), Turin

Steve MacFarlane, Michael Thomson and David Dickson at Ibstock Brick Ltd

Charlie Smith and his team at CI Smith Builders Glasgow

Jim Garvie and Colin Johnston at Angus College, Arbroath and the Apprentice Builders: Jake Black, Jay Butterworth, Callum Campbell, Cameron Campbell, Liam Crookston, Fraser Downie, John Gordon, Kyle Harris, Dean Heenan, Lee Knox, Drew Livingston and Jack McGregor

Dundee Contemporary Arts
152 Nethergate
Dundee
DD1 4DY

www.dca.org.uk

Scottish Charity no. SCO26631

Distribution Art Data

ISBN 978-0-9558769-6-7